D1105196

Changing Times
Ancient Greece

Entertainment

By Stewart Ross

Illustrated by Adam Hook

First published in 2007 by
Compass Point Books
3109 West 50th Street, #115
Minneapolis, MN 55410
Visit Compass Point Books on the Internet at *www.compasspointbooks.com*
or e-mail your request to *custserv@compasspointbooks.com*

Library of Congress Cataloging-in-Publication Data
Ross, Stewart.
  Ancient Greece entertainment / by Stewart Ross ; illustrations by Adam Hook.
    p. cm. — (Changing times)
  Includes bibliographical references and index.
  ISBN-13: 978-0-7565-2086-1 (library binding)
  ISBN-10: 0-7565-2086-X (library binding)
1. Amusements—Greece—History—To 1500—Juvenile literature.
I. Hook, Adam. II. Title. III. Series.

  GV21.R67 2006
  796.0938--dc22   2006027041

Picture Acknowledgments
The publishers would like to thank the following for permission to reproduce
their pictures:
Art Archive: 11 (Museo di Villa Giulia, Rome/Dagli Orti), 12 (Archaeological
Museum, Spina Ferrara/Dagli Orti [A]), 16 (Ephesus Archaeological Museum,
Selcuk, Turkey/Dagli Orti [A]), 19 (Archaeological Museum, Naples/Dagli
Orti), 20 (Museo Nazionale, Taranto/Dagli Orti), 22 (Dagli Orti), 24
(Archaeological Museum, Istanbul/Dagli Orti), 26 (National Archaeological
Museum, Athens/Dagli Orti), 28 (Musée du Louvre, Paris/Dagli Orti).
Bridgeman Art Library: 6 (Bonhams, London), 9 (British Museum, London), 14
(Ashmolean Museum, University of Oxford).

Contents

Introduction

Who Were the Ancient Greeks?

The ancient Greeks were a remarkable people who helped lay the foundations of our civilization. They lived in what is now Greece, on the surrounding Mediterranean islands, and on the neighboring coast of Asia Minor.

Ancient Greek civilization began on the island of Crete in about 2000 B.C. Spreading to the mainland, it reached its height during the Classical Period (480–330 B.C.). It lost political independence in about 150 B.C. to the Roman empire but played a major role in shaping Roman life.

The ancient Greeks lived in small, independent city-states. Each one consisted of a city and its surrounding farmland. The most powerful city-states were Attica (Athens) and Laconia (Sparta), a tough soldier-state. The Athenians were rich traders whose influence extended across the Mediterranean Sea. Their city was also a center for the arts and learning. It was home to some of the finest thinkers, writers, and artists the world has ever seen. The Athenians wrote and performed the first plays and developed the idea of democratic government. It is largely because of them that we remember the ancient Greeks today.

Entertainment in Ancient Greece

The ancient Greeks certainly knew how to enjoy themselves. Both children and adults played a wide range of sports and games. They also played instruments, sang, and told wonderful stories that still delight us today. And they invented two forms of entertainment that are still enjoyed: track and field competitions and theater. But it is important to remember that no large-scale entertainment was put on just for fun. In ancient Greece, games and plays were part of religious festivals held to honor what the Greeks believed were powerful gods and goddesses—the Greeks, like most ancient people, were deeply religious.

During the Classical Period, Athens was by far the most important and wealthy of the city-states. A good deal more is known about it than the other city-states. The Athenians were great writers who left an impressive collection of histories, plays, poems, letters, speeches, and philosophy.

Quotations from the philosophers Plato and Aristotle; the orators Demosthenes and Isocrates; the playwrights Aristophanes and Euripedes; the poets Homer and Pindar; the historians Herodotus, Thucydides, and Xenophon; and the writer Pausinias, help form a fascinating picture of entertainment in ancient Greece.

Toys and Games

The Greeks were great thinkers. Their philosophers had strong views on how children should be brought up, and all agreed that young people needed to be kept busy. Not surprisingly, archaeologists have found a wide range of ancient Greek toys and dolls. Although the technology is not as advanced as our own, many of the items are similar to those enjoyed today.

A collection of bronze animals from ancient Greece includes a deer, a boar, and a mythical beast known as a griffin.

Strepsiades: I also know that I formerly obeyed you, a lisping child of six years old, and bought you a go-cart ... with the first obolus I received from the Heliaea.
ARISTOPHANES, *CLOUDS*

obolus: ancient Greek coins

The cart mentioned here is a children's version of the adult chariot, the Greeks' swiftest and most exciting means of transport. It was common to give children carts and other presents at the time of the Diasia festival, which honored the goddess Hera. This was one of the handful of festivals in which children were encouraged to take part.

Babies shook rattles to keep themselves amused, an idea approved by the great philosopher Aristotle. Older children played with dolls. These were made of wood, cloth, or pottery, and some had movable limbs. Other popular toys were balls, hoops, model animals, and marbles.

were others standing about them and looking on.

a game of odd-and-even in a corner ... and there

> [The boys] were all playing at knuckle-bones and wearing their finest attire. Most ... were playing ... out-of-doors; but some were at a game of odd-and-even in a corner ... and there were others standing about them and looking on.
>
> PLATO, *LYSIS*

knuckle-bones, odd-and-even: two traditional games played by children

Knucklebones was played by throwing little bones into the air and catching them on the back of the hand. Children and adults loved betting on how they would land. They believed that fortune was decided by their gods and goddesses, so a correct forecast was a sign of a deity's favor. Ball games, juggling, and leapfrog were enjoyed by adults and children.

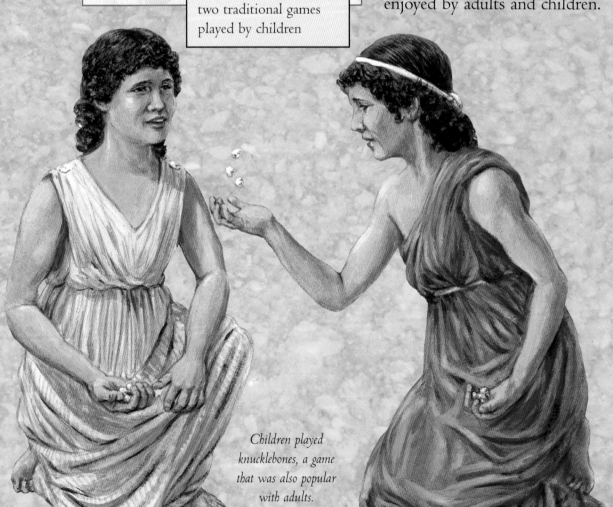

Children played knucklebones, a game that was also popular with adults.

Parties

The Greeks loved social gatherings with a lot of food, drinks, and entertainment. Their parties had one distinctive feature, especially among the citizens of Athens: they were rarely attended by husbands and wives together. Male and female members of the same family lived in different parts of the house and ate separate meals. A husband held a party for his friends and a wife for hers. We cannot be sure whether this was the same all over Greece, however, because most of our written evidence comes from Athens.

Two women chatted at a social gathering in the women's upstairs rooms.

Chorus: No, I have no passion for battles; what I love, is to drink with good comrades in the corner by the fire when good dry wood ... is crackling ...
ARISTOPHANES, PEACE

comrades: friends

Life in ancient Greece was physically very difficult. There were no laborsaving devices, most travel was on foot, and, when called on to do so, all men were expected to be warriors. So, as Aristophanes says, at the end of a hard day there was nothing better than to relax before a blazing fire. After a hearty evening meal of bread, fish, olives, and fruit, the Greeks relished a good fireside chat.

they betook them to drinking.

> [W]hen Socrates had taken his place and had dined with the rest, they made libation and sang a chant to the god ... as custom bids, till they betook them to drinking.
>
> PLATO, *SYMPOSIUM*

made libation: offered or drank liquid as a tribute or sacrifice
chant: song, hymn
betook them to: started

The most popular entertainment at home was the symposium, a formal dinner party held by a man at his house for his male friends. As Plato tells us, it began with a meal. This was accompanied by musicians, dancers, and other entertainers. Then came singing in praise of Dionysus, the god of new life, and perhaps a few games would be played. Finally, after the slaves had cleared away the dishes, the serious part of the evening began. Having elected a chairperson to guide their conversation, the guests drank wine and discussed serious and lighthearted topics long into the balmy Mediterranean night.

Greek men at a symposium played kottabos, *a game that involved throwing at a target.*

Hunting and Fishing

By the Classical Period, few Greek citizens regularly hunted wild animals for food. Even so, hunting was still a very popular sport. Everyone knew the story of Hercules slaying the terrifying Nemean lion, but since lions were almost extinct in the Mediterranean region, wolves and bears were now the most dangerous animals to pursue.

Most families, especially those living on the many islands of the Aegean, Ionian, and Mediterranean seas, lived along the coastline. Many others lived near the country's lakes or broad rivers. Because meat was expensive, fish was an important source of food. For many men, fishing was a job, a way of making a living and feeding the family.

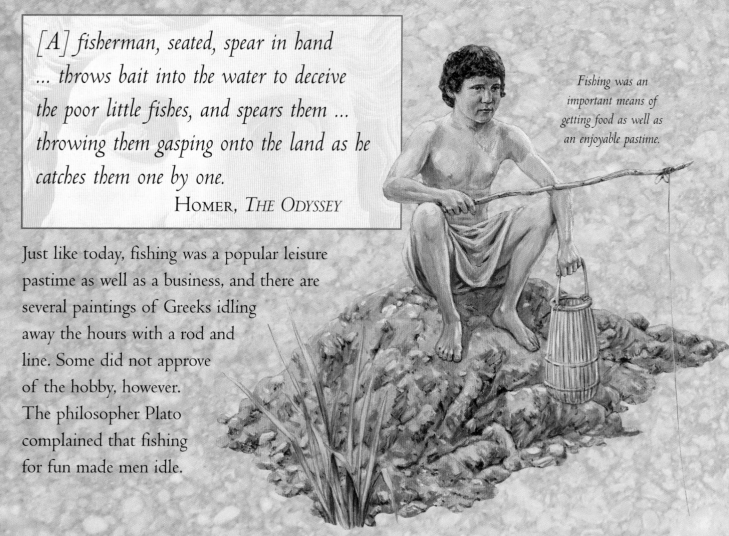

> *[A] fisherman, seated, spear in hand ... throws bait into the water to deceive the poor little fishes, and spears them ... throwing them gasping onto the land as he catches them one by one.*
>
> HOMER, *THE ODYSSEY*

Fishing was an important means of getting food as well as an enjoyable pastime.

Just like today, fishing was a popular leisure pastime as well as a business, and there are several paintings of Greeks idling away the hours with a rod and line. Some did not approve of the hobby, however. The philosopher Plato complained that fishing for fun made men idle.

> [M]y advice to the
> young is, do not despise
> hunting ... if you desire
> to grow up to be good
> men ... in war ...
> thought, word, and deed.
> XENOPHON, *ON HUNTING*

Xenophon praises hunting for its practical benefits. He thought all boys should hunt to improve their warrior qualities: fitness, speed of reaction, and bravery. The chief game animals were wild boar, deer, and hares, while partridges, quail, larks, ducks, and geese were the favorite game birds. Huntsmen used traps, spears, slings, and bows and arrows to capture prey. Horrifyingly, the Spartans went even further. Those who hoped to become part of the secret police (Krypteia) were sent to the countryside alone and instructed to kill any peasant farmers (helots) they encountered in the night.

Helped by his dogs, a hunter finally caught the deer he had been chasing.

Art

Art was tremendously important to the ancient Greeks. However, because so little remains, it is difficult to be sure what it was like. Buildings have been destroyed, pottery has been smashed, bronze statues have been melted down, and wooden statues have rotted away. Painting has suffered most, leaving the impression that it was unimportant. In fact, the opposite is true. Buildings like the Parthenon that today are blindingly white were, when built, a riot of brightly colored paintwork.

A glimpse of the perfect world: an elaborate fourth-century vase painted with scenes of hunting

And as when a man overlays silver with gold, a cunning workman ... and full of grace is the work he produces.
HOMER, *THE ODYSSEY*

To the Greeks, art was something beautiful, clever, or interesting made by the human hand. Homer is saying that the best art was even more than that: it was a glimpse of the perfect world of the gods and goddesses. In other words, art was linked to religion. Temples, such as Athena's on the Acropolis at Athens, were made as beautiful as possible to honor the goddess. An artist wanting to show perfect female beauty produced an image of Aphrodite, the goddess of love and beauty.

work he produces.

Here also are buried ... Nicias the son of Nicomedes, the best painter from life of all his contemporaries.

PAUSINIAS, DESCRIPTION OF GREECE

contemporaries: people living at the same time

A sculptor skillfully revealed the goddess Aphrodite within a block of solid marble.

Although painting was only one of the many art forms pursued in ancient Athens, painters were well-respected. During the Classical Period, Athenians were also regarded as the region's finest architects, sculptors, and potters. Greek art and design remains influential to this day. Not all Greek art was noble and religious. On vases and dishes, for example, are lively and amusing paintings of everyday people and animals.

Music and Dance

The Greeks believed music was central to civilized life. All citizens were expected to learn to play an instrument, sing, and dance as part of their basic education. Many of the great legendary heroes—Achilles, for instance—were said to be able musicians.

The word *music* comes from the Muses, nine mythical daughters of Zeus who inspired arts and sciences. The supposed power of music is best shown in the story of Orpheus, a son of Apollo, whose magical lute playing charmed rocks, monsters, and even Pluto, the god of the underworld.

> *Can we find a better than the traditional sort? —and this has two divisions, gymnastic for the body, and music for the soul ... And the young should be trained in both kinds.*
>
> SOCRATES IN PLATO'S *REPUBLIC*

A female musician played a type of flute with two pipes.

Here Socrates is explaining just why music was so important. More than just a pleasant sound, it showed the rhythm, balance, and harmony that everyone needed for a good life. Given the importance of music, it is not surprising to find it playing a major part in all religious festivals. Hymns were sung at mystery rituals in honor of the goddess Demeter. These were probably more restrained than the wilder rhythms and dancing at events honoring the fertility god Dionysus.

dance ... to increase the suppleness of his body.

> [N]o part of his
> [the Syracusan
> boy's] body was idle
> during the dance, but
> neck, legs, and hands were all
> active together. And that is the way a
> person must dance ... to increase the
> suppleness of his body.
>
> SOCRATES IN XENOPHON'S,
> SYMPOSIUM

suppleness: limber

The Greeks loved to dance. Three main instruments provided the music: the kithara, a form of lyre; the *aulos*, a wind instrument somewhere between a flute and an oboe; and the tambourine. The kithara, supposed to have been invented in an idle moment by Hermes, messenger to the gods, was the king of instruments. Pictures also show musicians playing drums, harps, and panpipes (a gift from Hermes' son Pan).

A woman danced at a festival honoring the god Dionysus.

Poetry

For centuries before they wrote them down, the Greeks composed and sang a wide variety of songs. This tradition continued long after writing had been invented. In fact, nearly all Greek poetry was meant to be sung in public, and there was often little difference between a poem and a song.

The person—man or woman—who performed a poem to his or her own music was much respected, and there may once even have been a special poets' school on the island of Chios. Later, Athens held competitions for poets who wrote epics, which are long poems that tell stories about heroic events.

> *Epic poetry ... and the poetry of tragic drama ... these ... may all be said to be "representations of life."*
>
> ARISTOTLE, *POETICS*

epic poetry: stories in the form of poems

The philosopher Aristotle presents the main types of Greek poetry. Epic poems from the eighth century B.C., like Homer's poems *The Iliad* and *The Odyssey*, are among the earliest works of Greek literature still surviving. They were written with a particular rhythm, each line being a hexameter, with six groups of two or three syllables.

The poet Menander (342?–292? B.C.) was the witty author of more than a hundred plays.

16

The poetry of drama grew out of the chants, known as *dithyrambs*, that choruses sang at festivals. Lighter poems, often love songs, and comic poems, popular at symposia, sometimes stirred great emotion in their audiences.

A Greek poet read his latest work.

> *Chorus: [O]ur poet of to-day is likewise worthy of this favor ... he dares to tell the truth, he boldly braves both waterspouts and hurricanes.*
>
> ARISTOPHANES, *KNIGHTS*

waterspouts: tornadoes over water

The ancient Greek poets had a special role. It was their job to remind people of the great deeds and characters of the past and to point out the errors of the present—in other words, to keep alive the virtues that made Greece great. Hesiod, for example, author of some of the earliest Greek poems, constantly reminds his audience of the need to be honorable and to reach their full potential.

worthy of this favor ... he dares to tell the truth, he boldly braves both waterspouts and hurricanes.

Storytelling

The Greeks were fine storytellers. Perhaps best known are their famous myths and legends featuring characters such as Hercules, the Amazons, and the terrible man-bull creature, the Minotaur. These stories have had a huge impact on our culture, influencing writers such as William Shakespeare and J. K. Rowling, the author of the Harry Potter series. Greek scholars were also among the first to try to separate mythical and legendary tales from factual history. We could say, therefore, that they were the fathers of the modern subject of history.

The battles described in Homer's Iliad *still have the power to thrill, more than 2,500 years later.*

An angry man—there is my story: the bitter rancor of Achilles, prince of the house of Peleus, which brought a thousand troubles upon the Achaian host.

HOMER, *ILIAD*

rancor: ill will
host: army

With these words, Homer begins his *Iliad*, one of the most enthralling tales ever told. It tells how Queen Helen of Sparta was carried away to the city of Troy and how an army of Greek warriors fought to avenge this insult. The Trojan horse—the trick by which the Greeks eventually entered the city—is one of the most famous images in our culture. We even name a part of our bodies, the Achilles tendon, after the Greek warrior whose only weak spot was his heel.

troubles upon the Achaian host.

Herodotus (485?–425? B.C.), the traveler and writer whose fascinating Histories *is still widely read.*

In this book, the result of my inquiries into history, I hope to do two things: to preserve the memory of the past ... both our own and of the Asiatic peoples ... and ... to show how the two races came into conflict.

HERODOTUS, THE HISTORIES

Herodotus wrote at length in prose. He also set out his material carefully and logically and tried to check that the information he gave was accurate. His *Histories* tells the story of Greece's long wars with Persia, enlivened with thoughts and observations from his many travels. Greece's next great conflict, the civil wars stemming from the rivalry between Athens and Sparta, was brilliantly reported by Thucydides, another fine early historian.

Festivals

Greece's many festivals—Athens alone had more than 120 annually—were public religious celebrations equivalent to our holidays. They also gave people a break from work and an excuse to have fun. Most festivals were in three parts: a procession, a sacrifice, and a feast. Athletic festivals, such as the famous Olympic Games, were also organized in honor of a deity. A handful of festivals were Panhellenic (involving all of Greece), but the majority were celebrated in a single city-state.

A vase painting shows figures dancing at a festival in Tarentum, a Greek colony in southern Italy.

[Athenians] provide plenty of means for the mind to refresh itself from business. We celebrate games and sacrifices all the year round ...

THUCYDIDES, *THE HISTORY OF THE PELOPONNESIAN WAR*

Thanks to Athenian writers, we know most about the festivals of Athens. Each summer a festival called the Panathenaea was held to honor Athena, the city's goddess, during which the citizens presented her with a new robe. Dionysus had two festivals. The Rural Dionysia, held in the countryside in December, involved a riotous procession and much celebration. The main event of the Great Dionysia, held in the city in March, was a famous drama competition. The Thargelia festival, held in the late spring, honored Apollo, while the Thesmophoria was a women's festival held in the autumn to honor Demeter, the harvest goddess.

At [Athens'] festivals ... every man among you knows long beforehand ... what he is to receive, when and from whom he is to receive it, and what he is to do; nothing here is left to chance ...
DEMOSTHENES, *SPEECHES*

The pipe-playing god Pan inspired festivals in many rural areas of ancient Greece.

Ancient Greek festivals, which sometimes went on for several days, were important for the city's economy. The poor often received free food and drink, and the huge sums spent on decorations, statues, and processions greatly helped local painters, musicians, sculptors, and poets. Athletic festivals also played a part in keeping the population fit.

The Theater

Festivals in honor of Dionysus had a procession in which a chorus danced and sang. Around 534 B.C. a festival organizer named Thespis introduced a single player alongside the chorus, and the theater was born. The player, or actor, was later joined by two other men, who acted out a drama. In time, performances were given in specially built theaters, with a stage for the actors and a space in front of it—the orchestra—for the chorus.

> [T]here exists no "freedom of speech" except that which is enjoyed ... in the theatre by the comic poets.
>
> ISOCRATES,
> ON THE PEACE

The Greek theater at Epidaurus seated 12,000 people, all of whom could hear the actors clearly, thanks to the theater's superb design.

In addition to enjoying the freedoms noted by Isocrates, some Greek playwrights were authors of the greatest ability. It is not easy for us to judge because fewer than 50 complete plays survive, but the most able and popular playwrights seem to have been Aeschylus, Sophocles, Euripides, and Aristophanes. All plays performed during the Great Dionysia festival were judged by a panel of citizens. Prizes were awarded to the best producer, actor, and playwright (called a poet).

a crowd of thieves prowling around it.

> *Let us begin by handing over all this gear to the care of our servants, for no place is less safe than a theatre; there is always a crowd of thieves prowling around it ...*
>
> LEADER OF THE CHORUS
> IN ARISTOPHANES' *PEACE*

Aristophanes pokes fun at the theater in which the play was being performed. It was situated in the heart of Athens, just below the Acropolis. It may well have been a haunt of thieves. Like all Greek theaters, it was carved out of a hillside. High above the stage, the audience had a perfect view and could hear every word.

Drama judges, seated on a special stone bench, discussed a play they had just seen.

Tragedy and Comedy

Most surviving Greek plays are either tragedies or comedies. Tragedies were exciting, serious plays usually retelling, in three episodes, a well-known story from mythology. The theme was often the fall of a once-noble person. Until about 400 B.C., comedies were rude fantasies that made fun of important citizens who thought too much of themselves. Later comedy was more realistic, more serious, and tended to mock society as a whole.

> Chorus: What men expect is not brought to pass, but a god finds a way to achieve the unexpected. Such is the outcome of this story.
>
> EURIPIDES, MEDEA

A carving made in honor of Euripides (484?–406? B.C.), the last great Greek writer of tragic dramas.

In this tragedy play, Medea, wife of Jason and mother of his children, takes ghastly revenge on her husband for his unfaithfulness. Euripides' words at the end of the terrifying play illustrate its tragic theme— our lives are in the hands of the gods, and struggle how we may, it is they, not we, who control events.

to pass, but a god finds a way to achieve the unexpected.

A potbellied actor in a comedy wore a mask typical of those worn in all Greek plays.

> *Xanthias: Shall I crack any of those old jokes, master, at which the audience never fails to laugh?*
> *Dionysus: Aye, what you will, except "I'm getting crushed": Fight shy of that: I'm sick of that already.*
>
> ARISTOPHANES,
> THE FROGS

Aristophanes' lines from the comedy *The Frogs* (so called because the chorus dressed as frogs) show the main purpose of his plays: to amuse the audience. The more they laughed, the better his chance of winning first prize. He was clearly good at his job, too—he won four first prizes and three seconds at the annual drama festival in Athens.

Such is the outcome of this story.

Sports

Competition, especially in sports, was in the Greeks' blood. Physical fitness was seen as very important. Countless sculptures and paintings show the perfect young man with a body like a god—beautiful, strong, fit, and ready for war. All citizens, young and not so young, aimed for this ideal. Larger cities had a gymnasium, or sports complex, that included baths, massage couches, training facilities, a running track, and outdoor wrestling grounds. The better-funded gymnasiums had teams of coaches, instructors, and other assistants available.

> *They were all off together at once, whipping up the horses, flicking them with the reins, crying them on furiously ...*
>
> HOMER, *THE ILIAD*

Chariot races were the most popular sporting events and were often held to round off a religious festival. The lightweight chariots, pulled at breakneck speed by teams of two or four horses, were made of painted wood and basketwork. Collisions were common, making a race extremely dangerous. The charioteers were hardened professionals who, if successful, could make their fortunes. Horse races were also popular, but since neither stirrups nor saddles had been invented, they were almost as dangerous.

A bronze statue features a young jockey on a leaping horse. Galloping without stirrups, which had yet to be invented, was not easy.

three of whom won a prize both as boys and men.

> *The disadvantages of excessive training in early years are amply proved by the list of Olympic victors, not more than two or three of whom won a prize both as boys and men.*
> ARISTOTLE, *POLITICS*

Although Aristotle may have disagreed, sports remained a key part of male citizens' education. Although Athenian girls had little opportunity for physical exercise, Spartan women were encouraged to be as fit as the men, and they did well in the female games (Heraia). Sports were held on track and field. Runners raced up and down a straight track, not an oval one. Field events included boxing, wrestling, discus and javelin throwing, and the standing-start long jump, in which the competitors swung weights to help them leap farther.

A young Spartan athlete sprinted for the finishing line. Spartan women were generally the most fit in Greece.

The Olympic Games

Four great sports festivals—the Pythian, Nemean, Isthmian, and Olympic Games—drew athletes and spectators from all across the Greek world. Held every fourth summer at Olympia, in the southwestern Peloponnese, the greatest of these sports festivals were the Olympic Games. They honored Zeus, king of the gods, and according to legend, they had been founded by Hercules.

Herakles portioned the booty, war's gift, made sacrifice and founded the fourth year's feast with the first Olympiad and the winning of victories.

PINDAR, ODES, OLYMPIAN X

Olympic champions were heroes. Although they earned no official prize money and were crowned only with laurel wreaths, victors were hailed as superstars in their home states. A mark of the Olympics' importance was the Olympic truce, which outlawed war near the site of the games and forbade executions to allow people to safely travel to the festivals. A golden statue of Zeus, 40 feet (12.2 meters) high, adorned the site's temple, and 100 oxen were sacrificed on the third day of the five-day festival.

Throwing the discus was one of the oldest sports and part of the ancient Greek pentathlon.

again with the same team of mares.

Cimon, the son of Stesagoras ... had the good fortune to win the chariot race at Olympia ... At the next games he won the prize again with the same team of mares.

HERODOTUS,
THE HISTORIES

A champion athlete was crowned with a wreath of laurels. There was nothing for those who came in second or third.

The triumphant Cimon was the owner, not the driver, of the winning chariot team. Because of the prestige earned by a victory, competition in all events was ferocious. Wrestlers and boxers were known to kill their opponents. Runners tripped opponents, and charioteers deliberately tried to overturn their rivals' chariots. Thankfully, when the Olympics were revived in 1896, the organizers overlooked the Games' unscrupulous side and focused instead on their noble ideals.

Timeline

All dates are B.C.

c. 2000	A Greek-style civilization appears on the island of Crete.
c. 1400	Greek civilization spreads to Mycenae on mainland Greece.
776	The first recorded Olympic Games.
c. 750–700	Homer creates his famous poems, *The Iliad* and *The Odyssey*.
c. 650	Classic Greek sculpture appears.
c. 600	"Black figure" vase painting appears.
534	Thespis introduces a single actor beside the chorus in his dramas.
c. 525	"Red figure" vase painting appears. The playwright Aeschylus is born.
c. 496	The playwright Sophocles is born.
490–479	Greece's wars with the Persian Empire inspire fine writing such as the work of Herodotus.
484	The historian Herodotus is born.
c. 480	The playwright Euripides is born.
c. 461	The "golden age" of Athens begins (to 431). Many great works of art and literature are produced.
461–446	Athens and Sparta fight to dominate Greece. Every fourth year the war stops for the Olympic truce, when the games are held.
c. 455	The historian Thucydides is born.
c. 450	The playwright Aristophanes is born.
446–431	Athens and Sparta agree on a temporary truce, and entertainments flourish once again.
431–404	The Peloponnesian War is fought.
404	Athens surrenders to Sparta. The victory of Sparta, whose citizens are not renowned for their culture, is a blow to Greek civilization.
336–323	Alexander the Great of Macedonia reigns. His conquests carry the Greek way of life as far as Asia.
146	Greece is absorbed into the Roman Empire. The Romans maintain many features of Greek life, including the celebrated Olympic Games.

Glossary

Difficult words from the quoted material appear beside each quotation panel. This glossary explains words used in the main text.

acropolis	A fort, often on a rocky hill, at the heart of a Greek city.
Aeschylus	A writer of tragic plays.
Apollo	The handsome god of music, prophesy, and archery.
archaeologist	One who looks for evidence of the past in physical remains, often by digging.
Aristophanes	A writer of comedies.
Aristotle	A scientist and philosopher.
Athena	The goddess of Athens, often associated with war, the arts, and crafts.
citizen	A privileged member of a city-state whose family has normally lived there for many generations.
city-state	A self-governing city with its surrounding farmland.
comedy	A play, often amusing, that dealt with ordinary people in everyday situations.
deity	A god or goddess.
Demeter	The goddess of corn and the harvest.
Dionysus	The god of wine and new life.
dithyramb	A hymn for dancing in honor of Dionysus.
economy	All the parts of a city's business and trade.
epic	A long poem celebrating great deeds of heroes.
Euripides	A writer of tragic plays.
Hermes	The messenger of the gods.
Herodotus	A historian of the wars between Greece and Persia.
hexameter	A line of poetry with syllables in six groups.
Homer	A poet who most scholars believe wrote the famous epic poems *The Iliad* and *The Odyssey*.
philosopher	Literally a person who "loves learning"; someone who tackles abstract questions, such as the meaning of justice.
ritual	Religious behavior or actions repeated at regular intervals.
sacrifice	Make an offering to a deity, often by killing a valuable animal.
Sophocles	A writer of tragic plays.
symposium	An all-male dinner party.
Thucydides	A historian of the wars between Athens and Sparta.
underworld	The place far under the earth where the spirits of the dead lived.
Zeus	The king of the gods.

Further Information

Further Reading

Connolly, Peter, and Andrew Solway. *Ancient Greece*. New York: Oxford University Press, 2001.

Dell, Pamela. *Socrates: Ancient Greek in Search of Truth*. Minneapolis: Compass Point Books, 2007.

Pearson, Anne. *Ancient Greece*. New York: Dorling Kindersley, 2004.

Roberts, Jennifer T., and Tracy Barrett. *Ancient Greek World*. New York: Oxford University Press, 2004.

On the Web

For more information on this topic, use FactHound.
1. Go to *www.facthound.com*
2. Type in this book ID: 075652086X
3. Click on the *Fetch It* button.

FactHound will find the best Web sites for you.

Index